Life + Soul
LIBRARY

Why do I have to say please and thank you?

Big issues for little people around behaviour and manners

Written by **Dr Emma Waddington** + **Dr Christopher McCurry**

Illustrated by **Louis Thomas**

Frances Lincoln
Children's Books

Contents

3 .... How to use this book

4-7 .... Introduction

8-9 .... Why do I have to say 'thank you'?

10-11 .... Why do I have to say 'please'?

12-13 .... Do I have to say 'I'm sorry' even when I'm not sorry?

14-15 .... Why do I have to look at you when you talk to me?

16-17 .... Why must I share?

18-19 .... Why must I wait my turn?

20-21 .... What is wrong with snatching if it's mine?

22-23 .... Why do I have to use a fork?

24-25 .... Why can't I say someone is fat if they *are* fat?

26-27 .... Why can't I hit Angus if he hits me?

28-29 .... Why can't I whine? What's wrong with whining?

30-31 .... Why must I kiss Granny?

32 .... Further reading and resources

How to use this book

This book has been conceived for you to share with a child. Each spread is themed by topic and should be used as a discussion point to help you to talk through common issues in childhood.

STEP 1   Turn to the spread featuring the issue you wish to discuss with a child. •

STEP 2   Before sitting down with the child, read the advice from the authors explaining some common causes of behavioural patterns, and some tips on how to tackle them. •

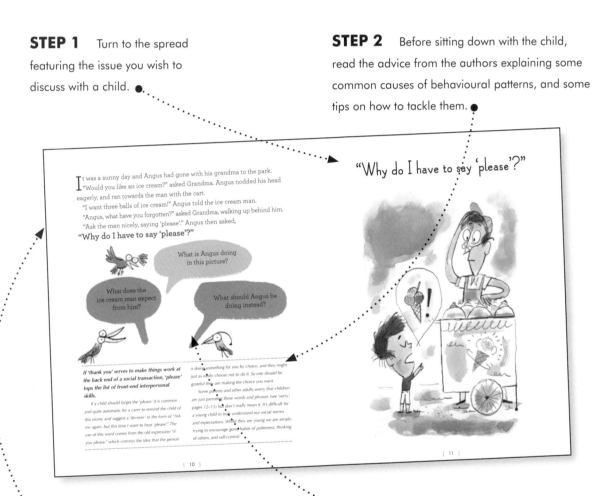

It was a sunny day and Angus had gone with his grandma to the park. "Would you like an ice cream?" asked Grandma. Angus nodded his head eagerly, and ran towards the man with the cart.
"I want three balls of ice cream!" Angus told the ice cream man.
"Angus, what have you forgotten?" asked Grandma, walking up behind him.
"Ask the man nicely, saying 'please'." Angus then asked,
"Why do I have to say 'please'?"

What is Angus doing in this picture?

What does the ice cream man expect from him?

What should Angus be doing instead?

If 'thank you' serves to make things work at the back end of a social transaction, 'please' tops the list of front-end interpersonal skills.
If a child should forget the 'please' it is common and quite automatic for a carer to remind the child of this nicely and suggest a 'do-over' in the form of "Ask me again, but this time I want to hear 'please'." The use of this word comes from the old expression "if you please," which conveys the idea that the person

is doing something for you by choice, and they might just as easily choose not to do it. So one should be grateful they are making the choice you want.
Some parents and other adults worry that children are just parroting these words and phrases (see 'sorry', pages 12–13) but don't really mean it. It's difficult for a young child to truly understand our social norms and expectations. When they are young we are simply trying to encourage good habits of politeness, thinking of others, and self-control.

"Why do I have to say 'please'?"

| 10 | | 11 |

STEP 3   Direct the child's attention to the illustration and read the story that accompanies the scenario in front of them. This is a safe and non-confrontational way to approach a topic.

STEP 4   Explore the issue further with the conversational prompts which encourage the child to empathise with the scenario. This should ease you in to having a conversation with them about their own behaviour.

"It's my birthday party and she gave me a fairy costume. I hate fairies! Why do I have to say thank you?" asked Olivia.

How will this book help you talk to a child?

Children love to ask questions. A four-year-old girl can reportedly ask up to 390 questions a day, which adds up to over 100,000 questions a year! Curiosity is an essential ingredient for a child's developing brain, and our response plays a key part in that development.

Most questions from children are pretty mundane, but now and again they will ask something that leaves us dumbfounded, surprised, or, at times, upset, meaning that we cannot answer without further thought and time. In this book, we will explain some commonly-asked questions from children, offer advice on how to respond (and explain why your answers matter!), and talk about how to manage the emotions that may come with these discussions. If you need further support in certain areas, turn to the back of this book where you will find resources to help you.

Why are children curious about their world?

Children are natural explorers. Exploring is a reflex when they are very young; they reach out and observe objects in their surroundings. As they grow and are able to move and manipulate their environment, exploring becomes more exciting and rewarding to them; they will poke, pick, chew, hit, throw, lick and grab just about anything that is around them!

Children independently seek to understand and discover their environment, which helps them develop theories and understandings of their world. As they explore and their brains grow, their

Children independently seek to understand and discover their environment

natural curiosity leads them to ask questions.

These early years are the most important for a child's brain, setting the ground for future growth. The brain is at its most receptive and it is learning faster and changing in response to new experiences more efficiently.

How is a child's behaviour connected to their developing brain?

As children explore and learn, they are building their brain – in particular, the front of their brains. This is the part that helps us make sense of our world. In adults, it is huge, and this allows us to override the reactive back of the brain in order to slow down, reason, evaluate and make sense of situations and experiences.

However, up to the age of four, it is the back of a child's brain that dominates. This back part of the brain – also known as our reptilian brain – is responsible for letting us know when something bad is happening and informing us that we need to run away. This is a reactive part of the brain that was once

essential for survival and is, by nature, very inflexible. This is why it can be so hard to calm a tantrum in full blast.

Unfortunately, the front and back of the brain are poorly connected – especially in the very young. So when the amygdala, the specific part of the reptilian brain responsible for emotions such as fear and anger, fires up, it is very hard to tame.

As carers, we want our children to develop the front of the brain, as this will help them manage their behaviour. This means that we can reason with them when they are in the midst of a fierce tantrum; we can ask them to wait, and they will, before jumping out onto the road, and so on.

So as children ask questions and hear your answers, these experiences are also shaping their brains – in particular, their frontal lobes. As they build these networks, our children will be better able to manage social situations, build stronger bonds and act in ways that bring them joy and happiness.

> We want our children to develop the front of their brain, as this will help them manage their behaviour

How does a child learn good behaviour?

We often joke with parents that we have a responsibility to 'civilize' our children, and with our hard work we shape them into socialised adults who can function in society. Although we say this in jest, there is an element of truth. Children don't see the point of being courteous with others when it's not in their immediate interest and tend to see events in terms of how it will affect them in very short-term and concrete ways. Similarly, young children struggle with the concept of delayed gratification: they cannot wait to get what they want, even if this means getting less in the long run. Some years ago, a study asked children aged four to wait before eating a marshmallow in order to get a second one. The vast majority couldn't and immediately ate the first marshmallow, thereby depriving themselves of the second. It is only from about age six that children begin to realise that patience would bring a reward.

This is why we think of good manners and other polite, prosocial behaviors as 'little

> ## Children don't see the point of being courteous when it's not in their immediate interest

acts of self control'; opportunities to practise thinking of others, patience and self-discipline. Even little gestures – screaming instead of hitting a brother, or being able to say please (albeit in a rather irritating whine) – are important and should be recognised as building blocks and opportunities to rehearse new skills: all steps in the right direction.

Why, as carers, should we worry about manners?

Ultimately, we feel a deep sense of responsibility to have our children accepted by the rest of the pack. From an evolutionary perspective, it was life threatening to be expelled from the pack, so we are hardwired to ensure that this never happens to our offspring.

In Joan Manuel Serrat's song, Esos Locos Bajitos, or Those Crazy Shorties, he talks tenderly of how we can find ourselves just telling them "no", "stop", "put that down", "be quiet" and "sit still" in a never-ending cycle. Serrat recognises that as carers, we need to pause, connect with our children, and nurture them.

This is so much easier to do when we are relaxed, happy and sleeping well. You may feel there is little hope of this in the early years. So what can we do? When we are upset at our child's behaviour, our own amygdala (in the back of the brain) will be firing, shutting down our ability to reason and to teach them to do things differently. So we need to take a moment to regroup, breathe deeply, become aware of our thoughts and judgments, and remember our values, what we really want for our children and what really matters. Then we connect with our kids and see this as a teachable moment.

Once we are in a place where we can create a teachable moment, what do we do? We will describe the process of 'do-overs'. It is a little like learning to play a piece of music: you keep repeating the section until you can play it without any mistakes. By asking the child to say or do it again, we are rewiring their brain into a pattern of good behaviour.

There are two steps to the process: first, connect and validate your child's emotion with sentences like, "I can see you're frustrated" or, "ouch, that must have hurt". Secondly, ask them to repeat what they did, minus the problematic bit.

We have an opportunity in these early years to set some good routines and habits that a child will maintain in their adult years. By finding ways to encourage their curiosity as they question the need for being considerate of others, we will be activating their brains in different ways.

"Do-overs" rewire a child's brain into a pattern of good behaviour

By giving them reasons that are consistent with what matters to them in that moment – and in the long run – we will be helping them find meaning to their actions.

By making them feel understood and heard, we will be helping you manage some of the emotions that arise.

By being consistent in your expectations, setting good routines, and modelling prosocial behavior yourself, you will be communicating the importance of these actions.

Together we will work on making you feel more confident in navigating the torrent of questions that we are faced with daily with commitment and care.

We look forward to working in this new way together!

"**A**bby! I have a present for you," called her dad. Presents! Abby came running over.

"What is it?" she asked, and from behind his back, her dad revealed... a lolly! Yummy! She grabbed it excitedly.

"That's not very nice, Abby. When someone gives you something, you know that you should say 'thank you'," reminded her dad. Abby replied,

"Why do I have to say 'thank you'?"

How would Abby's dad feel if she said thank you?

How do you think her dad feels?

Why do you think Abby won't say thank you?

Children who are grateful have more friends, better grades, and set higher goals for themselves.

We say "thank you" to let others know that we recognize and appreciate what they've done for us. Expressing gratitude makes us feel better. And a nice by-product is that it makes others want to help us even more. Young children will likely appreciate that reasoning above the others.

There are many ways one can express gratitude.

When receiving a compliment you might say, "You're very kind to say so", or when offered help, "That's very kind of you." It sounds a bit old-fashioned, but it can be a pleasant variant of the old "thank you" response. As with any of these courtesies and little acts of self-control we are addressing here, it is important for carers to model these behaviors themselves in everyday life, and to point out when others do as well.

"Why do I have to say 'thank you'?"

It was a sunny day and Angus had gone with his grandma to the park. "Would you like an ice cream?" asked Grandma. Angus nodded his head eagerly, and ran towards the man with the cart.

"I want three balls of ice cream!" Angus told the ice cream man.

"Angus, what have you forgotten?" asked Grandma, walking up behind him.

"Ask the man nicely, saying 'please'." Angus then asked,

"Why do I have to say 'please'?"

What is Angus doing in this picture?

What does the ice cream man expect from him?

What should Angus be doing instead?

If 'thank you' serves to make things work at the back end of a social transaction, 'please' tops the list of front-end interpersonal skills.

If a child should forget the 'please' it is common and quite automatic for a carer to remind the child of this nicety and suggest a 'do-over' in the form of "Ask me again, but this time I want to hear 'please'." The use of this word comes from the old expression "if you please," which conveys the idea that the person

is doing something for you by choice, and they might just as easily choose not to do it. So one should be grateful they are making the choice you want.

Some parents and other adults worry that children are just parroting these words and phrases (see 'sorry', pages 12–13) but don't really mean it. It's difficult for a young child to truly understand our social norms and expectations. Whilst they are young we are simply trying to encourage good habits of politeness, thinking of others, and self-control.

"Why do I have to say 'please'?"

Yuki was playing outside.

"What are you doing, Yuki?" asked Ibrahim, wandering over. She told him that she was playing dress-up with her doll. Ibrahim asked if he could join in.

"No," said Yuki. "You're a boy so you can't play." Ibrahim didn't think this was very fair, so he snatched Yuki's doll. Yuki started to cry.

"Ibrahim!" said the teacher, coming over. "That wasn't very nice. Give Yuki her doll back, and tell her that you're sorry." But Ibrahim wanted to know,

"Do I have to say 'I'm sorry', even when I'm not sorry?"

What is Ibrahim thinking?

How is Yuki feeling?

What would you do if you were in Ibrahim's place?

This is a tricky topic. Apologies can come in many forms; a verbal "I'm sorry", a gesture of reconciliation, making amends somehow.

Very young children will do 'repair work' after a falling-out with a parent that might take the form of a request or even a mild demand, "Read me a story, Daddy." The parent, only minutes beyond some argument or power struggle with this child, may not be 'in the mood' to read a story at that moment. But it is important for the caregiver to recognize this olive branch and do their best to accept it and help the relationship heal and move on.

Parents are often frustrated when a child's apology doesn't appear sincere. Often this can lead to power struggles where the parent insists the child repeat the apology but with a more sincere tone. This rarely works as the child is likely to become more irritated and less willing to play the social game. We apologize because it's expected and is a gift that helps us get back to where we were before (fore-give). Accept whatever apology the child is willing to give at the moment, when emotions are likely still running high, and work on tone later when things have cooled down.

"Do I have to say 'I'm sorry' even when I'm not sorry?"

Olivia was home from school and was drawing a dinosaur on her dad's tablet.

"Did you have a nice day, Olivia?" asked her mum, coming in.

"Uh-huh," answered Olivia, drawing the dinsaur's claws. Her mum asked her what she had done. "Not much," relied Olivia, adding in some big teeth.

"Olivia, please will you put down the tablet and look at me when I talk to you?" asked her mum. Olivia asked back,

"Why do I have to look at you when you talk to me?"

Do you think Olivia is listening to her mum?

How would her mum know she is listening?

Does Mum sometimes not look at you when you're talking?

Talking and listening make up a crucial, daily transaction between carer, parent and child.

It is important to teach children that the job of the listener is to 'take care of' the speaker. This means giving the speaker non-verbal messages that show the listener is, in fact, attentive and receiving what the speaker is giving. One can explain to a child that eye contact helps convey this message of attentiveness.

For some children, shy or naturally anxious ones especially, making eye contact can be quite painful. When a child feels they are in trouble, shame can make it difficult to look an adult in the eye. In fact, in some cultures such eye contact from child to adult might be considered rude. As with the apology, it is sometimes best to have the child's attention and allow them to receive your message than to insist on eye contact when this might be increasing a child's distress to the point where the message you're trying to deliver is overshadowed.

"Why do I have to look at you when you talk to me?"

A ngus was eating his ice cream in the park when his friend Lola came over and also ordered one. She asked Angus what flavours he had.

"Strawberry, mango and vanilla," replied Angus.

"I have mint, pistachio and chocolate. If you share yours with me, I'll share mine with you," said Lola. But Angus wanted to know,

"Why must I share?"

What is the ice cream man thinking?

What are Angus and Olivia doing?

How do you feel when others share with you?

By about age four, most children understand the idea of sharing but it is a challenge do it.

They are so very in the moment and will not likely be telling themselves "I'll get some, too" or "soon, it will be my turn" (see 'taking turns', pages 18–19). They simply feel the immediate pang of impending loss. Children don't need a great deal of explanation about sharing. A simple "It's a rule we follow so that everyone can have some" can suffice. Model sharing yourself: "Let's share this biscuit" and so on. Do a little prepping before a play date or other situations where sharing is expected: "Olivia will be here soon. So remember, we're going to be sharing your toys". Some children find it more tolerable to share their things if, before their friend comes over, the child can choose to put away a favourite or precious item that will not be shared during the play date. This can give your child a sense of control that makes it easier to be generous with the rest of their possessions.

"Why must I share?"

I brahim needed the bathroom. Outside the boys' room was a queue of some of his classmates. This made Ibrahim feel cross! He didn't want to wait because he was uncomfortable, so he barged his way to the front of the line.

"Ibrahim, you can't do that," said a teacher. "All the other boys are waiting nicely, so you have to wait your turn." Ibrahim asked,

"Why must I wait my turn?"

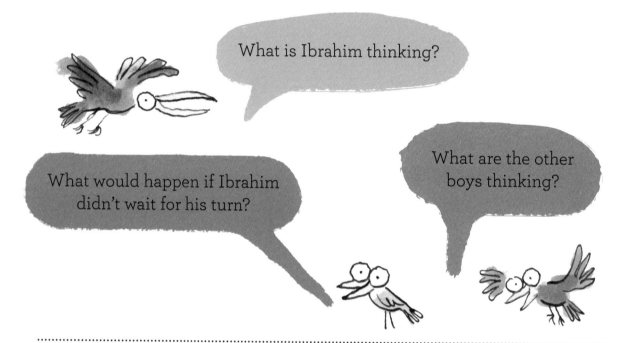

What is Ibrahim thinking?

What would happen if Ibrahim didn't wait for his turn?

What are the other boys thinking?

Taking turns or waiting your turn are integral to successful social interaction.

This may be the first context in which a child will show some willingness, however tenuous, to demonstrate patience. If getting on with classmates is important enough, the child will exercise that level of self-control. These little acts of self-control are important for developing a raft of competencies including impulse control, attention (in the form of maintaining focus instead of dwelling on immediate desires), perspective taking and time management to the extent that waiting your turn is in some way time-bound. Point out to the child that turn-taking is just one of the rules of being fair. Young children will understand the idea of 'rules' before they appreciate more social-emotional reasons such as "Tim feels sad when you push in." As with sharing, model and point out turn-taking as you go through daily life: when you are playing games, at the market, playing at the park, doing chores and so on.

"Why must I wait my turn?"

Angus was playing football with Ibrahim and some of his other friends. Ibrahim was really good at football and soon his team had two goals, while Angus's had scored nil. Angus got so cross about losing that he decided he'd had enough of the game. He picked up his ball and marched off.

"You can't snatch the ball away, we haven't finished the game!" said one of the other boys. Angus asked,

"What is wrong with snatching if it's mine?"

What is Angus doing?

What are the rest of the boys thinking?

Do you think they will want to play with him next time?

Much of what we've been describing is impulse control, and snatching – or refraining from snatching – is another example.

The foundation for impulse control is the development of those frontal lobes of the brain, so one should expect more control with age. Another big part of gaining control over our behavior is the development of language: the ability to talk oneself through a situation and not just react. When a child snatches something, it is often a good opportunity for a 'do-over'. Also, remember to do the validation piece, "Ah, you really want your ball back from Ibrahim. We use words to ask for what we want. Let's do that over, this time using your words." You may need to prompt the child as to what (simple) words to say. Assess the situation to see if the child will cooperate with a do-over and indeed give the ball back once your child uses their words. If that seems unlikely, or if your child is balking at the idea of a do-over, then it may not be a teachable moment. Avoid power struggles.

I brahim was at home and it was dinner time. He was really hungry after playing football all afternoon.

"Steak, chips and peas!" said Ibrahim's dad. What a treat! Ibrahim was so excited that he forgot his manners and began to gobble up his dinner with his hands.

"Ibrahim, what are you doing?" said Dad. "Use your knife and fork to eat properly, please." Ibrahim asked,

"Why do I have to use a fork?"

What does it look like to see Ibrahim eating like that?

Why don't you think Ibrahim is using a fork?

Do you ever seen grown-ups eat without forks?

Basic table manners, again, are another opportunity to practise little acts of patience, thoughtfulness of others, and self-control.

Using utensils, napkins, and sipping, rather than gulping, all involve slowing down and savouring the food and time together at the table. You can explain to the child that forks and spoons serve several purposes. They keep otherwise hot and messy foods from our fingers and hands, which is neater and cleaner (a value some children may not subscribe to). Table manners allow us to slow down the eating process, which aids digestion and enjoyment. When all else fails, simply state that it is a rule and an expectation, not just in your family, but in the wider social world generally. Some foods (sandwiches, for example) are meant to be eaten by hand. Some situations (a picnic) may have different rules and expectations than others (dining at a fancy restaurant). Carers need to help children recognise contextual cues and utilize them in order to know how one should behave.

"Why do I have to use a fork?"

Abby was going for a walk in the woods with her mum and dad and some of their friends, who had a son called William. She was very good at exploring in the woods and often spotted things that the grown-ups hadn't seen.

"Abby, why don't you take William exploring with you?" suggested Mum.

"I'm not taking William!" said Abby. "He's too fat."

"That isn't nice, Abby. You mustn't call people fat," said Mum. Abby asked,

"Why can't I say someone is fat if they *are* fat?"

Why do you think Abby has said the boy is fat?

Has anyone ever called you names?

How is the little boy feeling?

Some children do not have good filters. They say whatever comes to mind in whatever situation they are in.

Young children are often literal and unaware of social norms. This can result in embarrassing comments or remarks. As the carer, it is important to maintain your composure in these situations and not unnecessarily generate distress, confusion or embarrassment in the child. After all, the child likely feels they are just making an honest observation. It's best to avoid generating defensiveness and resistance to hearing your message. That message might be something along the lines of "Many people are sensitive about their appearance and it is best to not make such comments, especially when that person might hear them."

The situation would be quite different, of course, if one thought the child was being intentionally rude. That would require a stern reprimand and a restating of the family values of kindness and respect.

"Why can't I say someone is fat if they *are* fat?"

I brahim was in the school playground, playing tag with his friends. Ibrahim was good at tag – he was a fast runner – but after lots of running around, he was finally caught by his friend Angus.

"Tag! You're it!" shouted Angus, and he punched Ibrahim hard on the shoulder as he said it. Ibrahim didn't like this and hit Angus back.

A teacher came over to see what was going on. "Ibrahim! Did you hit Angus?" she asked. "You know that isn't allowed." Ibrahim asked,

"Why can't I hit Angus if he hits me?"

What is happening in this picture?

How do you think the situation will end?

Who will be happy? Who will be upset?

Young children tend to be deeply concerned with fairness. After all, we have been talking about sharing and taking turns. Why not take turns hitting each other?

When I (CM) was a child, my brother, John, and I would say, "He hit me back first!" But my parents never accepted this defence and we were both admonished for fighting.

It's impossible for a carer to monitor the goings-on of children with complete attention and adults may not always know who started what. It's best to not get into taking sides in these situations but to simply separate squabbling children for a period of time until things can be redirected to a less conflicted activity.

You may need to acknowledge that, yes, it isn't fair that you've been hit and you're not allowed to retaliate. But hitting just leads to more hitting and we need to solve problems through words and seeking help from an adult if words appear to not be working.

"Why can't I hit Angus if he hits me?"

Angus had gone into town with his mum, who had some things she needed to buy.

"Muuuuum," said Angus. "Can I have some sweets?"

"No, Angus," she said. "It's nearly lunchtime. I don't want you to fill up on sweets."

"But Mum! Please? Pleeease! I really want some sweets. Muuuuuuuum!" said Angus, and burst into tears.

Angus's mum sighed. "Angus, don't whine," she said. Through his tears, Angus asked his mum,

"Why can't I whine. What's wrong with whining?"

What is Angus's mum thinking?

How will it all end? Will Angus get what he wants?

Why is Angus holding on to her leg?

A basic assumption in these pages is that children, through their behaviour, are just trying to get their needs met.

These needs (for attention, security, feeling good about themselves, and so on) are legitimate and necessary. What matters is how the child is going about trying to get that particular need met. When a child acts in a manner that is not acceptable, it is important to consider what they might be trying to achieve and then give the child a chance to get their need met in a more prosocial manner. Hence, the 'do-over' with a 'positive opposite' behaviour; in this case a 'pleasant voice'. This may not always be possible, as when even the most pleasant voice cannot obtain what the child wants in the moment, such as a later bedtime or another piece of cake. But there will likely be many opportunities as with 'thank you' and 'please' to try again with a more pleasant tone. And, as with 'thank you' and 'please', using a pleasant voice will make it more likely that others will help you.

"Why can't I whine?
What's wrong with whining?"

A
bby's grandma had come to stay. She lived a long way away and only came to see Abby's family once a year.

"Hello, Abigail!" said Abby's grandma as she came into the house. "How's my little princess? Come and give me a kiss."

Abby couldn't really remember the last time she had seen her grandma. She felt a bit scared and stayed over by her dad.

"Abby, give Grandma a kiss," prompted her dad, but Abby asked,

"Why must I kiss Grandma?"

Why does Abby's grandma want a kiss?

Do you ever have to do things you don't like for others?

What is it that Abby doesn't like?

Some children may find some social behaviours strange or uncomfortable.

The young child who sees a grandparent only once a year may feel nervous or even repelled by this aged person who is behaving with such intimacy towards them. It's best to anticipate these events and give the child a little 'inoculation' around what to expect. Give the child some ideas about what will happen and, importantly, how the child is likely to think and feel. This is not 'setting the child up' to feel anxious or unhappy, quite the opposite; by matter-of-factly predicting certain ideas or feelings, it can make those experiences, should they arise, less alarming. For example, "When Grandma gets here she's going to be so happy to see you and she's going to want to give you a hug and a kiss. Grannies love to hug and kiss their grandchildren when they first see them. You might feel a bit scared, but it will be okay. Just give her a kiss on the cheek and then you can play. Which cheek will you pick to kiss, the left or the right?"

"Why must I kiss Grandma?"

Further reading and resources

Books to read with children

Bardhan-Quallen, S. *The Mine-O-Saur* (New York: Putnam Juvenile, 2007)

Crary, E. *Pick Up Your Socks... and Other Skills Growing Children Need!: A Practical Guide to Raising Responsible Children.* (Seattle, WA: Parenting Press, 1990)

Katz, K. *Excuse Me: A Little Book of Manners* (New York: Grosset & Dunlap, 2002)

Leaf, M. *How To Behave and Why* (Milford, C: Universe Publishing Co. Revised edition, 2002)

Websites

parents.com/kids/development/social/25-manners-kids-should-know/.
Parents.com, *25 Manners Kids Should Know From Parents*

parents.com/toddlers-preschoolers/development/manners/teaching-kids-to-mind-their-manners/.
Parents.com, *Teaching Kids to Mind Their Manners*

Why do I have to say please and thank you copyright © Frances Lincoln Ltd 2016
Text copyright © Dr Emma Waddington and Dr Christopher McCurry 2016
Illustrations copyright © Louis Thomas 2016

First published in the UK in 2016 by Frances Lincoln Children's Books,
74–77 White Lion Street, London N1 9PF, UK
QuartoKnows.com
Visit our blogs at QuartoKnows.com

A catalogue record for this book is available from the British Library.

ISBN 978-1-84780-796-0

Edited by Jenny Broom
Designed by Andrew Watson
Production by Laura Grandi
Published by Rachel Williams

Printed in China
1 3 5 7 9 8 6 4 2

MIX
Paper from
responsible sources
FSC
www.fsc.org
FSC® C104723